Journey to Olympia

The Story of the Olympic Games

By TESSA DUDER

ILLUSTRATIONS BY GRANT COLE

SCHOLASTIC INC.
New York Toronto London Auckland Sydney

Previously published in New Zealand by Ashton Scholastic Ltd.

ISBN 0-590-45796-9

Published by Scholastic Inc.,
730 Broadway, New York, NY 10003,
by arrangement with Ashton Scholastic Ltd.

12 11 10 9 8 7 6 5 4 3 2 1 2 3 4 5 6 7/9

Printed in the U.S.A. 08

First Scholastic printing, May 1992

CONTENTS

INTRODUCTION

You are a young athlete. A promising runner, perhaps, or a dedicated swimmer, a cyclist, a diver or a gymnast.

Maybe your chosen sport is judo, wrestling, weightlifting or boxing. Or maybe you prefer team games such as hockey, basketball, volleyball or soccer.

Do you like to compete in a canoe, or a rowing skiff or a yacht? Perhaps your special talent is for riding horses or archery or shooting.

These sports may each seem very different, but they have one thing in common. They are all included on the programme of the Olympic Games.

For a young athlete dreaming of success, an Olympic gold medal is the ultimate. There are other Games – European, Asian, Commonwealth, Pan-Pacific, Pan-American – and other world championships in many of these sports, but there is something very special about competing in an Olympic Games and winning an Olympic medal.

Why? What makes an Olympic gold medal so special? Or even a silver or bronze medal? Why do athletes train, either individually or with their teams, for many years just for the honour of even competing in the Olympic Games?

Every fourth year, sportsmen and women come from all over the world to take part in the Olympic Games. You may remember hearing about the Games held in Los Angeles, USA, in 1984, or in Seoul, South Korea, in 1988.

In 1992 they are being held in Barcelona, Spain. The 1996 Olympics in Atlanta, USA, will be particularly notable because they will mark one hundred years since the first Olympic Games were held in Athens, Greece, in 1896.

Well, not quite the *very* first! The Games in Athens were the first Olympics of the *modern* period of the

Games. In fact, the very first Olympic Games were held in Greece over 2800 years ago.

The Games at Olympia, or the *ancient* Olympics as they are usually called, were held every four years without a break for over a thousand years – from 776 BC to AD 395. More than 260 Games, or Olympiads, were held. They were so important to the ancient Greeks that they actually measured time by Olympiads.

We may sing of no contest greater than Olympia – wrote the famous poet Pindar – *just as water is the more precious of all the elements, just as gold is the most valuable of all goods, and just as the sun shines brighter than any other star, so shines Olympia, putting all other games into the shade.*

Whatever happened during those one thousand years, the Games at Olympia remained unaffected. There were many political changes and difficulties. Communities formed themselves into city states, often at war with their neighbours. Alexander the Great led an army into Persia, and even as far as India.

Many Greeks went to live outside Greece, in coastal ports around the Mediterranean, and in countries such as Egypt and Syria. Later, Greece even became a province of the Roman Empire – but whatever happened the Olympic Games seemed to continue regardless as a great national festival. Greek sculptors, poets and painters used their skills to sing the praises of the games and the athletes who competed there.

So the Olympics are the world's oldest and greatest sporting festival. This long, long tradition is one reason why Olympic glory is the dream of aspiring athletes. There are, however, several other reasons which are a little harder for us, who live almost in the twenty-first century, to understand.

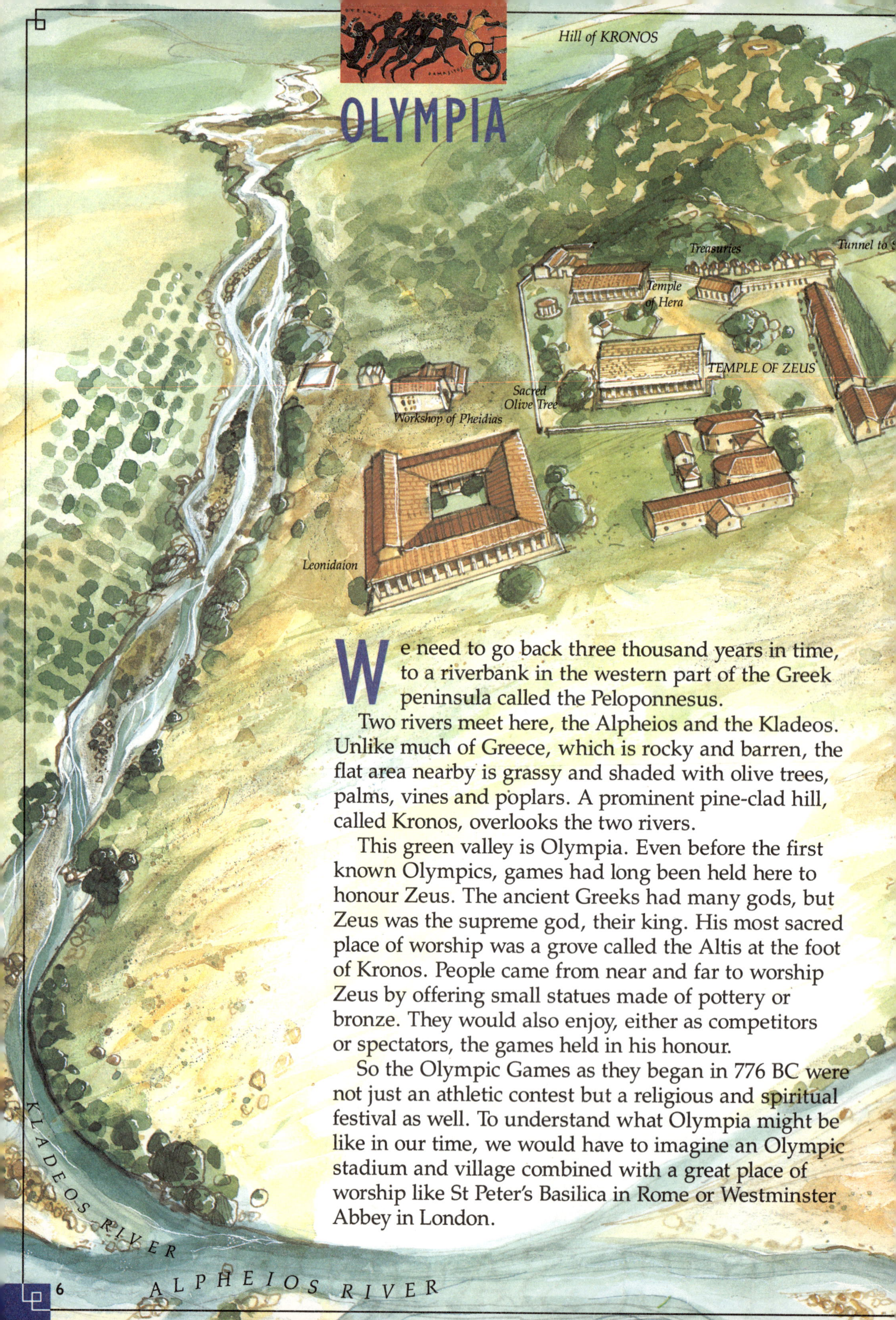

OLYMPIA

We need to go back three thousand years in time, to a riverbank in the western part of the Greek peninsula called the Peloponnesus.

Two rivers meet here, the Alpheios and the Kladeos. Unlike much of Greece, which is rocky and barren, the flat area nearby is grassy and shaded with olive trees, palms, vines and poplars. A prominent pine-clad hill, called Kronos, overlooks the two rivers.

This green valley is Olympia. Even before the first known Olympics, games had long been held here to honour Zeus. The ancient Greeks had many gods, but Zeus was the supreme god, their king. His most sacred place of worship was a grove called the Altis at the foot of Kronos. People came from near and far to worship Zeus by offering small statues made of pottery or bronze. They would also enjoy, either as competitors or spectators, the games held in his honour.

So the Olympic Games as they began in 776 BC were not just an athletic contest but a religious and spiritual festival as well. To understand what Olympia might be like in our time, we would have to imagine an Olympic stadium and village combined with a great place of worship like St Peter's Basilica in Rome or Westminster Abbey in London.

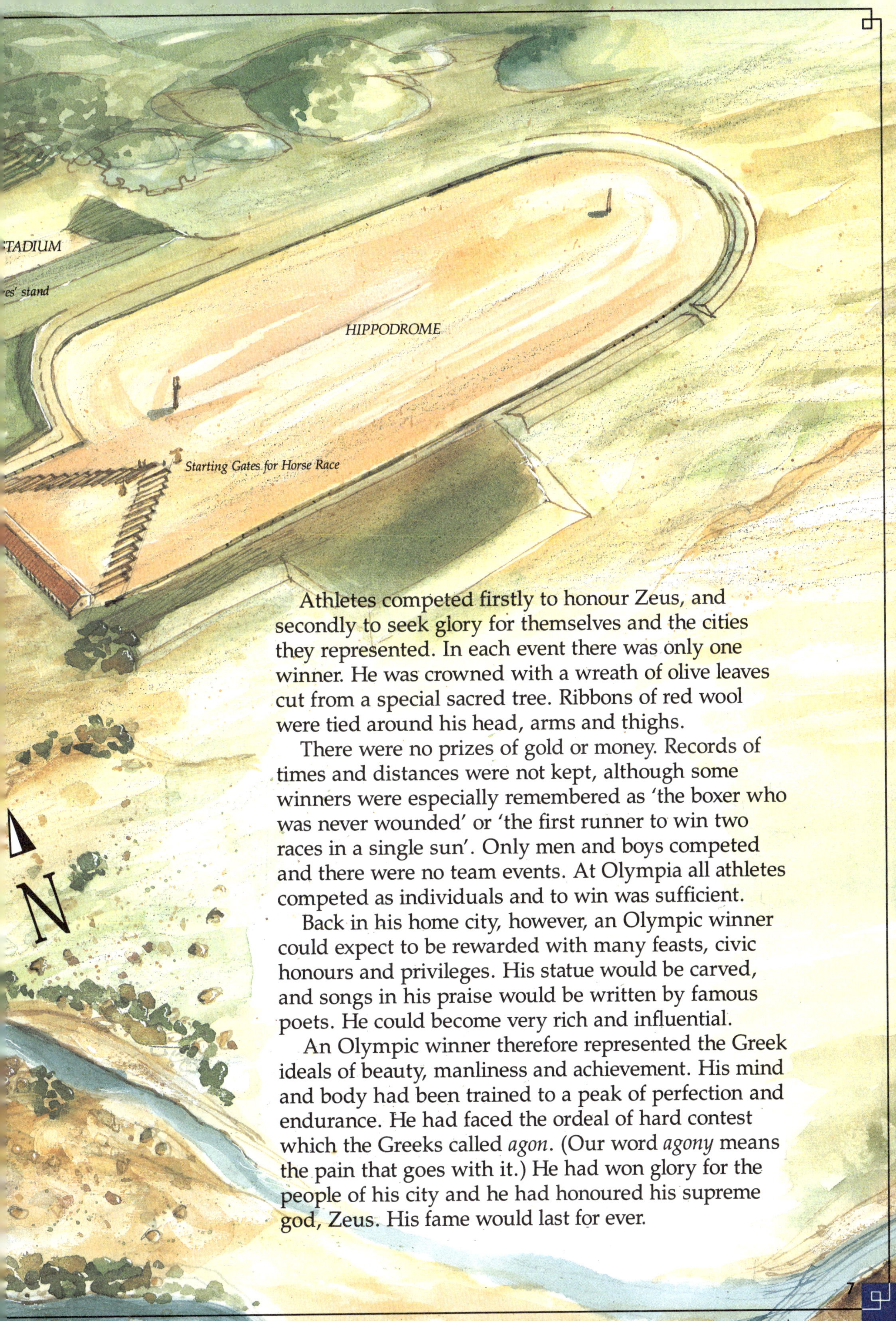

Athletes competed firstly to honour Zeus, and secondly to seek glory for themselves and the cities they represented. In each event there was only one winner. He was crowned with a wreath of olive leaves cut from a special sacred tree. Ribbons of red wool were tied around his head, arms and thighs.

There were no prizes of gold or money. Records of times and distances were not kept, although some winners were especially remembered as 'the boxer who was never wounded' or 'the first runner to win two races in a single sun'. Only men and boys competed and there were no team events. At Olympia all athletes competed as individuals and to win was sufficient.

Back in his home city, however, an Olympic winner could expect to be rewarded with many feasts, civic honours and privileges. His statue would be carved, and songs in his praise would be written by famous poets. He could become very rich and influential.

An Olympic winner therefore represented the Greek ideals of beauty, manliness and achievement. His mind and body had been trained to a peak of perfection and endurance. He had faced the ordeal of hard contest which the Greeks called *agon*. (Our word *agony* means the pain that goes with it.) He had won glory for the people of his city and he had honoured his supreme god, Zeus. His fame would last for ever.

HOW DO WE KNOW?

Well, of course, nothing lasts for ever, and even the ancient and famous Games at Olympia finally came to an end about AD 395, nearly 1600 years ago. Olympia, the Games, and all they stood for were forgotten for many centuries.

Then how do we know so much today about Olympia and the games that used to be held there every fourth year in mid-July, at the time of the full moon?

How do we know that a cook named Koroibos, from the nearby city of Elis, won the first 200-metre sprint race in 776 BC?

How do we know about the superman wrestler, Milo of Kroton, or the most famous runner of all, Leonidas of Rhodes? When he won three events at his fourth and last Olympics, bringing his total of olive wreaths to twelve, the people of Rhodes declared him a god!

How do we know about the athletes' training methods, their equipment, and the rules of competition? We know many details of the five-day programme, the roles of the judges and trainers, and that there was no admission fee for spectators. How do we know this?

How do we know about the hundreds of statues that once stood at Olympia, the altars and temples, the workshops, gymnasiums, guesthouses . . . even about the water supply?

Our knowledge comes from several sources:

Written records The first list of Olympic winners was compiled about 400 BC, providing valuable information for later writers whose work has survived. There are many references to Olympia and the Games in Greek literature, especially the victory hymns written by Pindar of Thebes. And a Greek historian called Pausanias visited Olympia in the second century AD and wrote the world's first guidebook to what he saw there.

Painted vases and pots, coins, bronze and marble statues, and friezes used to decorate buildings Many of these, dug from the ground by archaeologists, show athletes training and competing in different events. Decorated pottery, a speciality of painters from Athens, is especially full of wonderful details.

The ruins at Olympia itself For many hundreds of years, Olympia lay forgotten, devastated by earthquakes and floods and buried under four metres of river silt. Then, in 1776, an Englishman called Richard Chandler rediscovered the site of ancient Olympia. It was not until 1875, however, that archaeologists began to dig away the debris. They found the foundations and broken pillars of great marble buildings. From these they were able to establish the size, designs and purpose of the original buildings. Other finds were complete statues, shields, records inscribed on stone, and pottery.

From all this evidence, archaeologists and other scholars have begun to reconstruct models of Olympia, showing how it grew over many centuries and how it appeared to the many thousands of people who travelled there.

The five-day programme itself is less certain. Over the centuries, there were additions and changes. However, let's imagine ourselves back to the probable programme 2400 years ago, to Olympia at its height in the fourth century BC.

Let's go to Olympia for the Games!

JOURNEY TO OLYMPIA

About two months ago, heralds came to our city, proclaiming the Olympic truce and the time of the next Games. The truce means peace of a sort, for a time, between any cities who are fighting a war. Most of all it means that we, along with all the other people going to Olympia, can travel in safety.

We're going on foot across the Peloponnesus, but many people, especially Greeks living in other countries, will travel by sea and go by boat up the Alpheios river. They say Olympia itself is not so very far from the coast. (15 km in antiquity.)

After three long days on the road, we arrive at Olympia, very excited. You can't miss the hill of Kronos. It's not a big hill, but it stands apart, quite steep in places and covered with pine trees. Although we're tired and hungry, and the sun is still beating hot on our heads, we're going to go straight to the Altis, the Sanctuary right at the foot of Kronos, to the Temple of Zeus. There's not problem finding the way – we just join thousands of others heading towards the walls.

There are only men and boys, of course. Women are not allowed at Olympia, not during *the* Games anyway.

Well, we have seen quite a few, actually – singers and dancers – but only on the other side of the river.

With only one day to go before the opening ceremonies, the place is crowded and noisy. Now, passing through the gates, we can see the Temple of Zeus. It took ten years to build. The building is made entirely of white marble, with the roof supported by thirty-four massive columns, but some of the decorations just below the roof are coloured in bright blues, reds and gold.

There are many fine temples in Greece, but the statue inside is what we've *really* come to see – the statue of Zeus made by the famous sculptor Pheidias out of gold, ivory, ebony and precious stones. It's one of the Seven Wonders of the World . . . and little wonder. He is truly colossal. A man doesn't even come to his big toe! And if he stood up, he would go through the roof.

Now we've seen and honoured the god, we can explore the rest of the Altis. Nearby is the statue of Victory on her tall column, and over there is the old and very sacred olive tree which provides the leaves for the winners' crowns. The oldest temple is the temple to Hera. In front of that are two high altars where they make sacrifices of animals to the gods.

There are some trees in the sanctuary, but there are statues *everywhere*. Bronze ones of horses, marble ones of famous athletes. There are thousands of people, too, greeting friends or listening to the readings by philosophers and poets.

The stadium is next. People tell us that just beneath that row of small temples is the entrance to the stadium – but, they warn, only for the athletes and judges. So we walk over the embankment to get our first glimpse of the most famous stadium in all Greece.

The straight stretch of track has been broken up with picks and covered with white sand. We can see the stone sills where the athletes line up for the start of their events, and the small channel of drinking water for the spectators at the very edge of the track. The embankments on each side are not very high, but we're told there's room for 40,000 people.

We're really surprised, considering all the Olympiads that have been held here, at how plain the stadium is. Except for a small platform for the judges on one side, there are no seats – everyone stands here, or sits on the grass. If we walk along the top of one embankment we

can see down into the much bigger race-track they call the hippodrome, where the chariot and horse races are going to be held.

It is *hot*. We walk back beside the wall of the Altis towards the living and training areas of Olympia. That tall plain building is the actual workshop of Pheidias. These other fine buildings are not for ordinary folk, not even for the athletes. They're for official delegates sent from cities all over Greece, all trying to outdo each other in richness and splendour. We've got a tent, which we'll pitch down near the river *if* we can find a space, and we'll make a fire to cook our food.

We're told that the athletes and judges will arrive at dawn tomorrow from Elis (58 km away), where they have all been living for the past month. The training programme there is apparently very, *very* hard and strict. The athletes have to follow the programme set down by the judges, even down to what they eat!

And in the end, not even all the athletes are chosen. Imagine it – being selected by your city, training for the required ten months, coming to Elis . . . and then being judged unworthy to compete!

After our long journey we want to sleep well tonight, but the place is packed for miles around; it's noisy, dusty, and full of donkeys, horses, chariots, carts, people and flies. Merchants are everywhere, setting up stalls to sell food and other goods, including small

statues to offer to Zeus. Outside the main area there are some women in the crowd, selling flowers, singing and dancing.

We might have to walk quite a long way beside the river before we find a quiet spot. The flies are bad enough, but the mosquitos are *terrible*.

Tomorrow, at dawn, the official procession will arrive from Elis and the Games will begin.

DAY ONE

The official procession must be almost in sight, as there's a general commotion along the valley. We had set out early this morning, but not early enough. As the procession finally arrives in the Altis, we get only glimpses of the ten Olympic judges in their purple robes, behind them the athletes, charioteers, trainers, the boy athletes with their fathers and brothers, and richly dressed official guests.

Luckily, we are quite close to the Council House where the procession comes to a halt. Another statue of Zeus overlooks the scene as the athletes take solemn oaths that they will compete according to the rules of Olympia. The judges, who are men of Elis chosen by lot, also swear that they will judge fairly and in secret.

Inside the Council House the competitors in the horse events are being registered, and lots are drawn for events such as boxing and wrestling, which are fought off in pairs.

The last official ceremony today surprises us, because we didn't know that musicians could win Olympic wreaths. It's the contest for the trumpeters and heralds, to see whose trumpet note or voice carries the greatest distance. The winners will be the official trumpeters and announcers for the rest of the Games.

Now the procession breaks up. The athletes go to train and rest for tomorrow's contests, while the officials will meet and check that everything is ready. But there is still plenty for us to see, because in the Altis different groups are offering prayers and sacrifices to the gods. The horse owners are making special offerings to Poseidon, Hera, Pan and others, because the chariot races tomorrow morning are very dangerous events. No owner wants to see his horses or riders injured in a crash.

We find a shady spot under a tree where we sleep through the hottest hours of the day. Later in the afternoon we wander through the Altis, listening to speeches and poetry. We go inside the cool temple to admire the statue of Zeus for a second time. The excitement here is everything we expected it would be. We don't sleep very well that night, and imagine that the charioteers and athletes don't either.

DAY TWO

We arrive at the stadium before sunrise, but even so, we can only get a position at the very back of the embankment. Today are the boys' events.

People around us who've been to Olympia before tell us that the boy competitors are usually aged between twelve and eighteen. Surely, we say, that can't be fair. No, they say, not always, so the judges have the last word. They've been known to exclude young, undeveloped boys of twelve or thirteen who are still children, or very big boys of sixteen and seventeen who are virtually full-grown men. There have been several cases, however, where so-called boys, not allowed to compete as boys, have entered in the men's events and won!

Here they come now – the purple-robed officials and the young athletes. Most are youths, at that stage between child and man. As is the custom at all the Games, they are naked, their skins burnt dark brown during their months of training. They walk slowly and solemnly, trying to conceal their excitement, because this is Olympia.

Trumpet and voice proclaim the opening of the Games. First up is the stadion race – a sprint down the track. Heats first, then the final. The crowd goes mad, throwing flowers and branches to the victor as he is given his palm branch and is borne aloft on the shoulders of his countrymen. The boxing, wrestling and pankration (a sort of no-holds-barred wrestling) take many hours before the eventual winners are equally acclaimed. We are all getting extremely hot and sunburnt, so it is quite a relief when the boys' games finish late in the day and we can go back to our tent by the river.

Even from here we can hear the songs of victory celebrations late into the night. There will be some very proud fathers at Olympia tonight.

DAY THREE

This is the morning of the horse events. Even in the darkness, before the first light brightens the sky, the hippodrome is completely crowded with people.

From the top of the embankment we get a good view of the turning post at the eastern end, which is where, we think grimly, most of the accidents will probably happen. To begin with, all the horses and riders parade into the arena. The wooden chariots look so slender, we wonder how on earth they stay together when the horses are galloping at full speed. Or how the drivers endure the bumpy ride for so long.

Then we have the races – chariots drawn by four horses, followed by races just for full-grown horses, for mares and for foals. The judges, say our neighbours, decide what is a foal and what is a horse in much the same way as they do the boys and men for the athletics contests – on their appearance, and using common sense.

Three exciting chariot races complete the programme. The main races go round the track twelve times. Others make eight circuits, and the foals only three. As expected, there are several crashes near the turning posts at either end when the riders are jostling and competing for the inside position. Several horses and riders fall and are injured, but we hear afterwards that none were killed.

The most amazing thing is the way in which the chariot races are started. The riders draw lots to decide whether they will start in the inner or outer lanes. The outer riders go first, the middle one last. In theory they all get a fair start, but we think the horses on the outside have an advantage since they are already at full speed when the horses on the inside finally get going. Presumably, they can't think of any fairer way to do it.

Being on the north embankment, which is nearest to the stadium, we are in a handy position to run down and get a good place near the judges' stand for the pentathlon. This is probably the most difficult contest in the Olympiad. The athletes compete in the long jump, the discus, the javelin, the stadion race (200-metre sprint) and the wrestling.

The pentathletes are the best all-round athletes, because they have to be strong for the wrestling and discus throwing, and nimble for the running, jumping and javelin throwing.

The contest takes all afternoon and stretches the athletes to the limit. We all swelter in the scorching sun while the athletes prowl around waiting their turns for the various events. We watch them prepare to throw the heavy bronze discus, or get up speed before tossing the javelin, or concentrate on a perfect jump, remembering to throw away the hand weights just before they land. We are close enough to see when some are pleased with their efforts and others are disappointed or furious with themselves.

Finally, two are left: hard bronzed men, the oil on their bodies now mixed with dust and sand, moving slowly to conserve their strength as they prepare for the last and toughest contest, the wrestling.

Around us the excitement of the crowd has reached fever pitch. Both wrestlers are tired and determined, but one gradually gains the upper hand. Eventually, he is declared the winner and given the palm. He is carried high through the crowds.

At sundown, the end of a long day, we are happy to sit quietly a little way up Kronos, looking down on the Altis. The whole area is lit with torches as preparations are made to perform the sacred ceremonies in honour of Pelops, the legendary founder of the chariot races. The victors and other competitors — many of whom are nursing injuries — will be giving thanks.

DAY FOUR

During the night, the whole valley of Olympia turns silver under a full moon. When day breaks, the holiest day of all begins. Before any more races are held, the most important procession and ritual sacrifice to Zeus will take place.

Even as we approach the Altis, we can hear the low moans of the one hundred oxen that have been assembled for the sacrifice. Soon the procession approaches: official delegates and ambassadors from other cities and states dressed in their finest robes, carrying offerings of gold and silver; then come the judges, priests, athletes, officials, and finally, reluctantly, the oxen given by the people of Elis.

The oxen are slaughtered before the great altar of Zeus, a high structure composed of the remains of many previous sacrifices. A *hundred* oxen means a lot of blood and flies in the sun. The bodies are dragged away, except for the haunches which are cut off and carried to the top of the mound to be burned in honour of Zeus. It is said that he takes sustenance from the smoke.

Later tonight the rest of the ox flesh will be roasted for a public banquet.

Meantime, we go over to the stadium for more athletic events. Today is the special day for the runners, and there will also be the main wrestling, boxing and pankration contests.

By some good luck we've managed to squeeze into the crowd down near the finishing line for the 200-metre stadion race. As the athletes come through the special entrance the herald announces their names Their bodies shine with the oil of their final massage, and they all do exercises to warm up their muscles.

After drawing lots for positions, the sprinters line up with their feet on the marble slabs of the starting line at the far end. We can't hear the starting command, but we can see the athletes go tense and then burst away at high speed down the track. There are several heats to find twenty runners for the final.

The final race is over in a matter of seconds. Even from here we couldn't pick the winner. The judges cast their votes. Finally, the herald announces a name and the crowd goes wild. The stadion winner is special. His name will be given to this Olympiad, as the winner of the oldest race on the programme. A messenger has already left to jump into a chariot and speed back to the victor's home city with the news so that a great parade and feast can be arranged for his return.

Then there is another but longer sprint, the diaulos, up the track and back. This time the competitors start and finish from our end. The winner is often the man who turns most neatly and swiftly around the post at the far end.

Then we have the dolichos, the longest running race – twenty full lengths of the track. These runners are built quite differently to the sprinters. They have slender legs but well developed shoulders, so they can keep up the distance runner's rhythmic arm swing for much longer.

Next come the events which create pandemonium among the crowds: the wrestling, boxing and pankration. Many of these men are *huge* and have scars

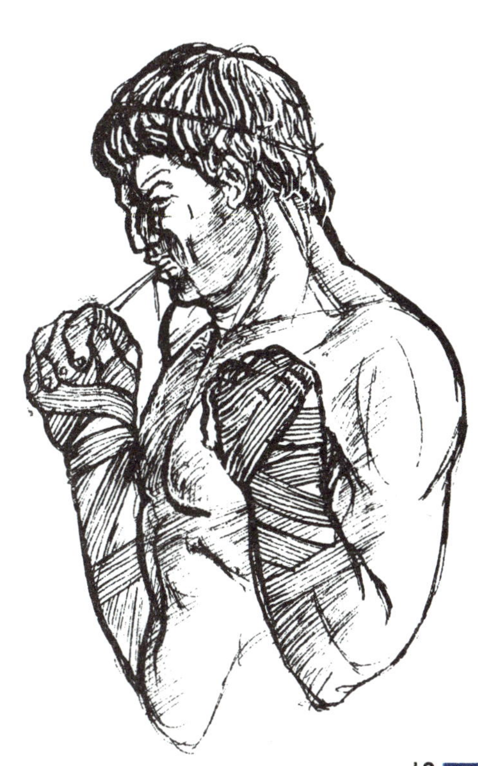

on their faces. The boxers look particularly fierce with their hands bound in a kind of padded leather glove. The bouts are sometimes very long and hard, sometimes short and one-sided. The crowd yells, laughs, jeers and whistles. After a lot of sweat and blood and noise, winners emerge.

The last event is the race in armour, two lengths of the track. It's said that this race is to remind all men that the primary purpose of keeping fit is for war. A set of twenty-five shields is kept in the temple of Zeus for this event. The runners also wear helmets and need a good sense of balance to be able to run with all this heavy, lopsided equipment.

What a day! We're all very badly sunburnt, and suffering from thirst. Our ears are pounding. The flies are bad, and tonight the mosquitos will be worse. But that's what you expect if you want to be a spectator at Olympia!

DAY FIVE

The games began with worship and finish with offerings and thanks to the gods. We start out *really* early this morning and are rewarded with a great view of the procession of winners in front of the temple of Zeus. As each winner's name and city are called by the herald, he comes forward to be crowned by the most senior judge with the wreath made of sacred olive leaves.

Sadly, for the spectators and unsuccessful athletes, this is the final event. The winners, however, will go on to a banquet given at noon by the people of Elis, the controllers of the Games.

Tonight there'll be many parties, especially among the friends and supporters of the winners. We'll have our own small party down by the river with the new friends we've met at Olympia.

Rich or poor, winners or losers, ambassadors or just spectators, most of us will be on our way home tomorrow. But even as spectators we can boast, back in our villages and towns: "*We've* been to an Olympiad!" Despite our sunburn and empty pockets, we intend to come again, in four years' time.

WOMEN AT OLYMPIA

This bronze figurine of a female runner probably comes from Sparta, where women were expected to take part in athletics.

The ancient festival at Olympia – which meant so much to all Greeks, and later to people from other countries as well – was a strictly male affair for its whole thousand years.

Pausanias, in his guidebook, writes of a precipitous mountain with lofty cliffs on the road to Olympia.

'It is a law of Elis that any woman who is discovered at the Olympic Games will be pitched headlong from this mountain.'

Strangely enough, he also says that young girls were apparently not refused entrance, and singers and dancers entertained the crowds on the outskirts of Olympia during the festival. At any other time, women could happily visit the Altis.

The judges, however, refused all suggestions that they follow the other major Greek games and include women's events. Instead, women had a festival of their own at Olympia, called the Games of Hera. These were also held every four years, with olive wreaths for the winners whose statues or paintings were then placed in the temple of Hera.

There was one event only, the foot race, slightly shorter than the Olympic stadion or sprint, and held for three different age groups. These games were also organised by the people of Elis, but compared to the Olympiad they were a very minor affair.

Although not allowed to compete at the Olympiad themselves, there was no rule to prevent women owners entering their horses. The most famous was Kyniska, wealthy daughter of King Archidamos of Sparta. Her team of horses won the chariot race twice in the fourth century BC. It is thought that she had a statue of herself erected in the Altis, with an inscription on the base which read:

Sparta's kings were fathers and brothers of mine
But since with my chariot and storming horses I, Kyniska,
Have won the prize, I place my effigy here
And proudly proclaim
That of all Grecian women I first bore the crown.

One other woman pushed her luck almost too far. She was Kallipateira, daughter of the famed boxer

Diagoras of Rhodes. Not only her father but also her three brothers had won Olympic crowns. When her husband died, she took over the training of her son, Pisirodos, and brought him to Olympia to compete. There was only one way to get into the stadium, and that was disguised as a male trainer. But she became so excited when her son won the boxing that she leapt out of the trainers' enclosure, lost her clothes and gave herself away.

Out of respect for her family, Kallipateira was not thrown from a lofty cliff, but from then on it was ruled that trainers had to be as naked as the athletes.

One woman was required to watch the Games, seated in splendid isolation in the stadium on a small marble altar opposite the judges' platform. She was a married woman from Elis in her role as the priestess of Demeter Chamyne, the goddess connected with vegetation and fertility.

THE END OF THE ANCIENT OLYMPICS

So far we have talked mainly about the ancient Olympic Games at their height. Athletes came to Olympia firstly to honour Zeus, and secondly to honour their cities. Political differences between cities were forgotton in the spirit of fair competition and the Olympic truce. However, around the fourth century BC the Olympic spirit was beginning to be influenced by other factors.

As the facilities at Olympia became ever grander, athletes were becoming more demanding and specialised. They began to credit themselves, not Zeus, for their victories. They began to train so intensely for only one event that they developed only those muscles needed, instead of developing the finely balanced body that was the Greek ideal.

Athletes had always been supported financially by their cities or by wealthy patrons, and they expected to be well rewarded when they won. However, winning had become so important to rival cities that they began to use the Olympics as a means of scoring political points. Athletes were made incredible promises and offers to spur them to success.

As Greek cities fought amongst themselves, the might and power of the Roman Empire was growing. Roman athletes were allowed to compete in the Olympic Games, ending centuries of tradition that only Greek citizens could compete. In AD 146 the Greek mainland became a province of the Roman Empire.

For Olympia, this was a mixed blessing. A Roman general not only looted Olympia's treasure to pay for a war, but even had the 175th Olympiad in 80 BC transferred to Rome! However, Roman emperors and generals also provided money for new buildings at Olympia. Their money and patronage helped to ensure that people still came to the Olympics in their thousands. The victors were still honoured, but now they were Roman and Egyptian as well as Greek.

The Games continued for only another two hundred years. In AD 267 Olympia was threatened with invasion

by a tribe from southern Russia. In despair, the people of Elis tried to protect the most sacred buildings by building a wall around them. Unfortunately, they tore down other buildings in the process.

About a hundred years later, the ancient Olympic Games finally came to an end. The Christian emperor Theodosius banned all pagan activities and later ordered the Altis to be destroyed by fire. The gold and ivory statue of Zeus was stolen and ended up in Istanbul before it, too, was destroyed by fire. Between the fifth and eighth centuries AD, earthquakes, invasion, floods and landslides completed the destruction of Olympia.

REVIVAL

The spirit of Olympia was not destroyed, however. In 1875, a hundred years after the rediscovery of the site of Olympia by Richard Chandler, full-scale excavations were begun by a team of German archaeologists.

Germany was involved because its new Kaiser, Wilhelm I, was fascinated by Olympia and its Games. As a young man, he had heard a famous German archaeologist, Professor Ernst Curtius, give a talk about Olympia. When he became Kaiser, Wilhelm persuaded the Greek government to let Professor Curtius supervise the excavation. The first major work took six years, but it continues to this day.

In the way that one thing leads to another, the first discoveries were reported by the German scientists and read by a French nobleman, Baron Pierre de Coubertin. Like the Kaiser before him, he became entranced with the ideals of the ancient Olympics. Now that the ancient site had been rediscovered, surely the actual Games and all the good things they stood for could be recreated too?

It took Baron de Coubertin three years to find the support he needed. The first modern Olympic Games were held in Athens in 1896 and judged to be a huge success. The second modern Games were held in Paris in 1900 – a huge failure.

The Games held in St Louis, USA, (1904) and London (1908) had major problems. The Stockholm Games in 1912 were somewhat better, but those scheduled for Berlin in 1916 were cancelled because of World War I. However, the modern Olympics have survived all kinds of political and financial strife. After World War II, the

The stone altar at Delphi, on which are carved the five rings symbolic of the quinquennial spacing of the games.

1948 Games in London and the 1952 Games in Helsinki were both judged successes and the Games' future appeared assured.

However, new and quite different problems have arisen. In recent Olympiads there have been incidents of terrorism, political boycotts, and, perhaps most seriously of all, the growing threat of the use of drugs that help athletes to achieve better performances and win medals unfairly. In addition, the two-week programme has become bigger and bigger, requiring more and more venues in each host city.

Satellite television now enables almost the whole world to watch the Games together. During the 1980s political problems were happily overcome so that in Seoul in 1988 nearly all the world's countries were represented in some way. Only in one other place – at the United Nations – do people from all countries come together.

Only at the Olympics are countries represented by people who are not politicians or wealthy dictators, but ordinary people who have a special talent for sport.

Olympic symbol

The Olympic symbol was invented by the ancient Greeks. The five rings, which appeared on an altar in Delphi, indicated that the Games were held every fifth year, allowing four full years between each festival.

Baron de Coubertin extended the idea further by stating that the five rings represented the five continents of the world. The colours he chose – blue, yellow, black, green and red on a white background – appear in the flags of the competing nations.

FAMOUS OLYMPIANS

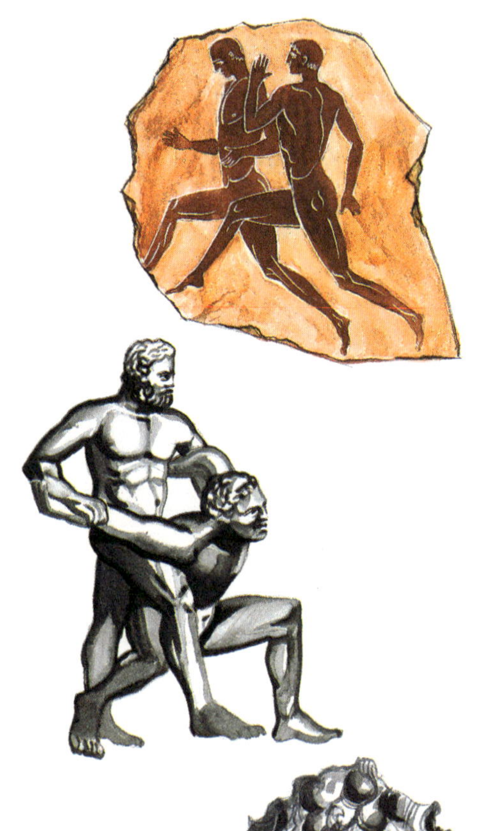

Leonidas of Rhodes

One of the greatest runners of all time, because he won three events (200 m, 400 m and the race in armour) in four successive Olympiads from 164 BC to 152 BC. That means he was the best runner for sixteen years, and was thirty-six years old when he won his final races. For a wrestler this would have been a great feat; for a runner, with his more sensitively trained body which is prone to muscle injury, it was unheard of and has never been equalled.

Milo of Kroton

A man of superhuman strength, Milo won the wrestling crown at Olympia five times. At his seventh and last Olympiad in 512 BC, and aged around forty, he was finally beaten by a man of twenty-eight. It was Milo, however, who was carried around the stadium in triumph, with his younger rival cheering as much as anyone.

Diagoras of Rhodes

Diagoras was renowned not only for his boxing but also for his sportsmanship and noble bearing. He won the crown at Olympia (464 BC) and many other games also. But he is also remembered as the founder of one of the greatest Olympic families. His sons, son-in-law and grandsons all won Olympic medals. He died, overcome with joy, during the victory ceremony for his two sons.

Jim Thorpe (USA)

A North American Indian, Jim Thorpe is the only athlete ever to win the Olympic double of the pentathlon (five events) and the decathlon (ten events) at the 1912 Games in Stockholm. A year later, Olympic officials decided that he was a professional because of small payments he had once accepted as a baseball player. He was stripped of his medals and records. In 1982, nearly thirty years after his death, Jim Thorpe's amateur status, medals and records were restored. He is once again recognised as one of the greatest athletes of the twentieth century.

Johnny Weissmuller (USA)

Hollywood's favourite 'Tarzan' of the 1930s was a former Olympic champion swimmer, Johnny Weissmuller. At the 1924 and 1928 Olympics he won five gold medals for freestyle, and a bronze in water polo. He held 25 official world records, including the 100 yards sprint for sixteen years, and when he retired from competition to become a film star, he had never once been beaten in a race.

Mildred (Babe) Didrikson (USA)

At the Los Angeles Olympics in 1932, Babe Didrikson from Texas won the 80 m hurdles and the javelin, and was placed second in the high jump. She was only eighteen. If the rules had allowed her to enter more than three events, she would probably have done equally as well in others. She is also remembered as a great natural athlete; accomplished in swimming, skating, shooting, rowing, soccer, basketball, tennis, and even boxing. After athletics, her most successful sport was golf, in which she won both the British and US national titles.

Paavo Nurmi (Finland)

Great athlete of the 1920s, Paavo Nurmi won a grand total of nine gold medals and three silvers and set 22 world records for distance running. At the 1924 Paris Olympics he was undefeated in seven events. He was one of the first athletes to approach running scientifically, training to beat the clock as well as his rivals.

Jesse Owens (USA)

Jesse Owens has been voted by some as the greatest athlete of the century. At the 1936 Games in Berlin, this young black man from Alabama spoiled Hitler's plan for German victories by winning both sprint events and the long jump, as well as helping the USA to win the 4 x 100 m relay. For the rest of his life, he was greatly respected as a tireless ambassador for sport.

Emil Zatopek (Czechslovakia)

At the 1952 Games in Helsinki, Emil Zatopek achieved an incredible triple win – the 5,000 metres, 10,000 metres and marathon. He was not a graceful runner but he trained harder than any others of his time. When he won the marathon at Helsinki, the crowd in the stadium gave him one of the greatest standing ovations an athlete has ever received.

Wilma Rudolph (USA)

Wilma Rudolph was one of a number of Olympic winners who overcame childhood illness to achieve fame. At age four, she contracted polio, scarlet fever and pneumonia, and it was doubtful that she would ever walk normally. Her left leg was in a brace for many years. At the age of thirteen, she was playing basketball; and at twenty she won three sprint titles at the 1960 Rome Olympics. She retired after setting an official world record in 1961.

Dawn Fraser (Australia)

The only swimmer ever to win the same event at three successive Olympics is the Australian Dawn Fraser in the 100 m freestyle. During her remarkable career she set 27 individual world records, took part in setting 12 relay records, and won 8 Olympic, 8 Commonwealth and 23 Australian titles. She was also the first woman to break the one-minute barrier for the 100 m freestyle. Dawn was the youngest of eight children and suffered from asthma. Although her swimming career ended abruptly with a ten-year ban from competition after one too many high-spirited pranks, she was awarded an MBE and eventually became a much-respected member of parliament in the Australian state of New South Wales.

Peter Snell (New Zealand)

At the Rome Olympics in 1960, an unknown Peter Snell came from nowhere to win the 800 metres title, defeating the world record-holder in the process. Four years later he achieved the impossible double' of the 800 metres and 1500 metres – thought to be impossible because of the stress of six strenuous races over eight days. A late starter to top-class athletics – he didn't compete seriously until he was 18 – Snell also set many world records for the mile, 800 metres, and 1500 metres.

Abebe Bikila (Ethiopia)

The first Olympic winner from black Africa, and first to win the Olympic marathon twice, Abebe Bikila was an unknown member of the Emperor Haile Selassie's bodyguard when he came to Rome in 1960. Running barefoot, he outclassed all opposition to set a world's best marathon time. Four years later, he repeated his success with similar ease, though just getting over an operation for appendicitis. Sadly, he had to retire injured from the 1968 Games and, tragically, saw the 1972 Games from a wheelchair, crippled after a car crash.

Bob Beamon (USA)

When 22-year-old Bob Beamon added over 21 inches to the world long jump record at the 1968 Mexico Olympics he almost fainted from the shock. His jump of 29ft 2½in (8.9m) was so fantastic that experts thought it would not be bettered until the 21st century. In fact, the record stood until the world athletic championships in Tokyo in August 1991, when both Mike Powell (USA) with a jump of 29ft 4½in (8.95m), and Carl Lewis (USA), with 29ft 2¾in (8.91m), broke Beamon's record.

Mark Spitz (USA)

At the 1968 Games in Mexico City, Californian Mark Spitz won two relay gold medals in swimming, but didn't quite live up to expectations in his individual events. By 1972 in Munich he was ready, and finished with seven golds – 100 m freestyle and 100 m butterfly, 200 m freestyle and 200 m butterfly, and three relay events – more golds in one sport in a single Olympics than any other competitor. What's more, all were in world record time! During his career, Spitz set a total of 25 individual world records, and was world Swimmer of the Year three times.

Nadia Comaneci (Romania)

In 1975 the world of gymnastics knew that Nadia Comaneci was an up-and-coming star. At the 1976 Olympics in Montreal, television audiences all around the world marvelled at the technical perfection, concentration and courage of the tiny 14-year-old, Nadia Comaneci, which saw her defeat the seemingly invincible Russians. She finished with three gold and one bronze individual medals, and a silver for her team. In 1980 she added two more individual golds, and the individual combined silver medal.

BIBLIOGRAPHY

Finley, M.I. and Pleket, W.W. *The Olympic Games: The First Thousand Years.* Chatto & Windus, London, 1976.

Yalouris, Nicolaos (ed.) *The Eternal Olympics: The Art and History of Sport.* Caratzas Brothers, New Rochelle, New York, 1979.

Swaddling, Judith *The Ancient Olympic Games.* Published for the Trustees of the British Museum by British Museum Publications Ltd, 1980.

Wallenschinsky, David *The Complete Book of the Olympics.* Penguin Books, Harmondsworth, Middlesex, England, 1984.